Sweetgrass and Other Poems

By
Joyce Keveren

SWEETGRASS AND OTHER POEMS
Copyright © 2022 by Joyce Keveren

All rights reserved. No part of this publication may be reproduced, distributed, or transmitted in any form or by any means, including photocopying, recording, or other electronic or mechanical methods, without the prior written permission of the publisher or author, except in the case of brief quotations embodied in critical reviews and certain other noncommercial uses permitted by copyright law.

Although every precaution has been taken to verify the accuracy of the information contained herein, the author and publisher assume no responsibility for any errors or omissions. No liability is assumed for damages that may result from the use of information contained within.

ISBN: Paperback: 978-1-63945-373-3
         ePub: 978-1-63945-374-0

Printed in the United States of America

Writers' Branding
1800-608-6550
www.writersbranding.com
orders@writersbranding.com

Contents

SECTION ONE: LOVE AND OTHER IDEAS 1

    SWEETGRASS 3
    LOSS 5
    SONORAN DESERT AUTUMN 6
    I MISS THE STARS 7
    JUNKIE LOVE 9
    LOVE (quite unrequited) 10
    SONORAN DESERT SPRING 11
    TO THE SAGUARO 12
    AWAKENING 14
    DAWN DREAMING 15
    MOON AND SEA YOU AND ME 16
    SPACE 17
    LOVE 18
    OUR FIRE 19
    MAGNETS 20
    THE WINNER 21
    THERE WILL BE NO SEQUEL 22
    LIFE CAN BE BRUTAL 23
    DIVORCE LOGIC 24
    THE NARCISSIST 25

MY DECLARATION OF INDEPENDENCE 26
MY PRAYER 27
TO A DOMESTIC TERRORIST 28
FOR EUGENE 29
A DUET.. 31
AT THE SEASHORE... 32
ANOTHER RACE THEORY 33

SECTION TWO: STATE OF THE UNION STUFF......... 35

GUILT 37
ADIOS 2021... 38
YET ANOTHER TRANSLATION 39
THE STARS... 40
TRY SOMETHING ELSE 41
BE PATIENT 43
WINNERS AND LOSERS 44
A 21st CENTURY CAUTIONARY TALE 45
SOME QUESTIONS 47
MORE QUESTIONS 49
GRAVITY 50
REQUIEM FOR A THIEF (Maybe our thief in chief) 52
ANOTHER QUESTION I DON'T HAVE THE ANSWER TO 53
21st CENTURY AMERICAN LAMENT 54
MIDNIGHT RAMBLING 56
DO NOT TURN AWAY... 57
AURORA BOREALIS 58
TALKING HEADS 2021 60
NOTES FROM THE PSYCH WARD 61
GENERATION GAP 63
MORE QUESTIONS 64
TO THE BILLIONAIRES.. 65
WINTER BLIZZARD... 67
REFLECTIONS 68
LESSONS WE CAN LEARN FROM THE FALL OF EMPIRES..... 69

SECTION THREE: WORLD OF WOMEN 73

 I RODE SHOTGUN 75
 MARRIAGE 76
 JUST ANOTHER KAREN 77
 ON LOWERING THE DIVORCE RATE 78
 IT'S ALL RELATIVE 79
 EARTH IS FEMALE TOO 80
 YOU ARE KNOWN BY THE COMPANY YOU KEEP 81
 LIFE ON EARTH 82

SECTION FOUR: 21ST CENTURY SONNETS 83

 SONNET # ONE 85
 SONNET # TWO 86
 SONNET # THREE 87
 SONNET # FOUR 88
 SONNET # FIVE 89
 SONNET # SIX 90
 SONNET # SEVEN 91
 SONNET # EIGHT -MIDNIGHT HOPELESSNESS 92
 SONNET # NINE - CHANGES 93
 SONNET # TEN - LOSS 94
 SONNET # ELEVEN - LIVING ON THE LINE 95
 SONNET # TWELVE - OMENS AND DREAMS 96
 ATTENTION SPANS 97

SECTION FIVE: HAIKU AND SENRYU 99

 TIME 101
 DIVINE RIGHT? 101
 HOMO SAPIENS 101
 LEMONS, LEMONS, LEMONS 101
 CLUES 102
 JANUARY 2021 102

LOVE	102
LOVE	102
CLICHES	103
THE LINE'S NOT BUSY	103
THEY'RE ALL MADE UP	103
LOVE	103
ADVICE	104
THE SYCOPHANT	104
NARCISSITIC PERSONALITY DISORDER	104
MORE NPD	105
LOVE	105
LOVE	105
REINCARNATION	105
MARRIAGE	106
21st CENTURY AFFLUENZA	106
LOVE	106
DO THE MATH	106
DO THE MATH (TWO)	107
LOVE	107
SOAPS TOO	107
LOVE	108
LOVE	108
CONFUSION	108
2020- ME TOO	109
HEALTH CARE PLAN	109
ELECTION 2020	109
WHITE SUPREMACY?	109
OR MONEY	110
POLITICS	110
MORE POLITICS	110
LOVE	110
URINOLOGY 101	111
NO TWO ALIKE	111
RELIGION	111
RELIGION 101	111
ANOTHER 110 DEGREE DAY	112

SOS	112
PHILOSOPHY 101	112
MORE SOS	112
OBVIOUSLY	113
LOVE ETC.	113
MARRIAGE	113
POLITICS	113
MORE LOVE	114
RAIN	114
MAYBE	114
CITY SOUNDS	114
A QUESTION	115
MAYBE OVERTIME	115
SOME OF IT MINE	115
THEOLOGY 101	115
DIVORCE	116
THEOLOGY 101	116
MORE THEOLOGY	116
I'M WITH STUPID	116
PHILOSOPHY 101	117
POLITICS	117
OR A LION	117
SOS	117
RELIGION	118
EASILY AND OFTEN	118
PEACE	118
JANUARY 6, 2021	118
SHOPPING	119
TURN OVER THOSE MONEY TABLES	119
DUST BUNNIES?	119
DARWIN WAS RIGHT	119
I STOLE THIS FROM CICERO. SORRY	120
THE TRUTH WILL SET YOU FREE	120
DAWN	120
LOVE	120
EINSTEIN SAID IT (or something like it)	121

LET US SPEAK THIS INTO EXISTENCE	121
WHITE SUPREMACY, FALLACIES, IDIOCIES AND TRUTH	121
LOVE	122
LOVE	122
THE LEADER	122
ILLUSION	122
GRATITUDE	123
GO AWAY	123
THINK FOR YOURSELF	123
A QUESTION	124
21st CENTURY POLITICS	124
DICTATORS	124
POLITICS	124
VOLTAIRE SAID IT TOO	125
ANOTHER QUESTION	125
MORE PHILOSOPHY	125
TO A CONGRESSMAN	125
LOVE	126
RACE THEORY	126
E=MC2	126
SEX	126
GIVE ME A MEMORY I CAN USE -ADELE-	127
TRANS-PORTATION	127
LOVE	127
LOVE	128
LOVE	128
MY PRAYER	128
FOOD	128
CHANGES	129
PROTECTION	129
EQUIVOCATION	129
MARRIAGE	129
BORDERS	130
THANK YOU, TREES	130
MUSIC	130
FOURTH OF JULY	130

MORE FOURTH OF JULY	131
MORE FOURTH OF JULY	131
MORE FOURTH OF JULY	131
MORE FOURTH OF JULY	131
MORE FOURTH OF JULY	132
CITIES	132
OUR BLUE WORLD	132
OUR WORLD	132
THE USA 21st CENTURY	133
THE WORLD 21st CENTURY	133
OUR CAMPFIRE SUN	133
SUN WORSHIPERS	133
SECURITY	134
AND B.S. TOO	134
USA 21ST CENTURY	134
MORE USA 21ST CENTURY	134
MORE USA 21ST CENTURY	135
THINK FOR YOURSELF	135
TEN OF THEM?	135
REALITY 101	136
MORE REALITY	136
THE LITTLE ONES	136
PROGRESS??	136
USA 21st CENTURY	137
USA 21st CENTURY	137
CAPITALISM 101	137
TIME TRAVEL	137
USA 21st CENTURY	138
USA 21ST CENTURY	138
DESMOND TUTU 2021	138
REPLACEMENT THEORY	139
AGAIN?	139
FROM THE IDIOT'S HANDBOOK	139
DAYBREAK	139
GAMBLERS ANONYMOUS-HEADS UP	140
LOVE	140

A QUESTION 140
TO A COWBOY... 140
GLOBALIZATION 141
THE OLYMPICS 141
MEMORIES 141
AT FIRST SIGHT 141
EGO TRIPPING 142
IMPOSTER 142
FORREST GUMP'S MOM WAS RIGHT 142
TEQUILA WISDOM.. 142
VIEWPOINTS.. 143
BUT IT'S YOUR DUST AND YOUR CHICKENS 143
THE TRUTH.. 143
RELIGION 144

SECTION SIX: SIX WORD STORIES 145

21st CENTURY POLITICS 147
21st CENTURY LOVE 147
THE WANT ADS... 147
SPORTS 147
GAMBLING 148
SPORTS 148
LOVE 148
THE END 149

x

SECTION ONE
LOVE AND OTHER IDEAS

SWEETGRASS

I am from the plains
The high northern plains
Where the sweetgrass
Bends to the will of the wind
And time stands still
In the long bitter winter
When snow covers the land
And small things hide.

I am of the plains
The rich grass covered plains
That give way to the range
 Of mountains where the snows
and the rains that feed
the prairie are born
and the summers are cool and kind.

I am from the pine covered hills
Of the north land
Where I ran wild
As a child
With a sky full of stars
To remind me –

I am from the plains
Where my love still remains
Lonely but remembered.

When the smell of the sweetgrass
Is on the wind,
I know I am nearly home.

LOSS

I think of you
On summer nights
When the air is still
And the sheets are hot.
I dream you're here
 And wake to find you're not.

SONORAN DESERT AUTUMN

Now the desert's in autumn
And that breeze from the south
Just the temperature of my skin is
Touching my face so gently,
I want to take my clothes off
So my whole body can feel that caress.

Déjà vu, I thought of you—
I always wanted to take off my clothes
Anytime I was near you, too—
Like that breeze, for that caress.

I MISS THE STARS

I miss the stars
Here in this city
Though I like the light
That made them fade.

I miss the stars
I've known forever
Arranged in those same
Patterns of light and delight;
Cassiopeia's chair, the Pleaides,
The Big Dipper that points
To the North Star,
Our unchanging sign of stability
That shows us the way.

Orion is now a dim, but loved
Reminder of the blazing warrior
 Of the northern plains
Where I was born.

I miss the scattered light
Of the Milky Way,
That sacred spiral
We call home
Where we live
Where I belong.

I miss the stars
I've known forever
From time to time
And life to life.
I love the city whose
Light dares to challenge
Those campfires in the sky
Where I can go in dreams,
But I miss the stars.

JUNKIE LOVE

They met in drug treatment
While kicking a heroin habit.
When love reached out to them,
They decided to grab it.
Now it's three years later.
She wipes up his puke
Can't wake him up
Injects Narcan into his thigh.
He falls asleep in her arms
And pisses the bed
So she washes the sheets
And then hits the streets
To get money for their next high.
Still, love is love
And love is good.

LOVE (QUITE UNREQUITED)

I fell in love with cocaine
At first snort
Couldn't get enough
Of that wonderful blow.
My life, which had been on hold
And oh, so unbearably slow
Suddenly took off
Like a rocket to hell
And I had no way to abort.
My head felt like a
Hot air balloon
Floating above all that
Stuff that I hated
And then I had an epiphany—
Reality is overrated!
The next thing I could see
Was how easily
I could kill myself
With this beautiful snow,
But it wouldn't matter
Because the world belongs to me
And I'll leave it to you

When I go.
But I know
The only thing
Worth anything
Is love. And cocaine, of course.

SONORAN DESERT SPRING

It is spring in my desert,
The flaming red bougainvillea
Is blooming with a fierceness
Equal to its dangerous thorns
And the yellow blossoms
Of the palo verde cover
My backyard so I'm
Walking on flower petals
While we wait for the rain.

TO THE SAGUARO

Saguaro
The sentinel
Guardian of the desert,
I know you move
When I close my eyes
And turn away.
Speak to me,
Tell me your secrets
Tell me your plan
Tell me your history,
Tell me what languages
You understand; Yaqui,
Spanish, French, English,
Tohono o otam, Apache,
Pima, Hohokam, perhaps a bit
Of Hopi or Navajo?
Can you bring the rains,
Calm the storms and divert the
Lightening from your
Tall old ones? I know you try.
You're a conservationist
Saving precious water,
You're a minimalist,
Needing little to survive,
A warrior and a peacemaker,
A pacifist, the Sonoran Gandhi,
Even your thorns
Practice passive resistance.

You are a dwelling place,
Giving shade, comfort and
Shelter to small creatures.
You give freely;
I can eat your fruit
And drink from your water supply.
You are royalty;
Your crown is of fruit and flowers.
You are a reminder
And a conduit of the Spirit.
My friend and teacher,
Do not leave me.

AWAKENING

You come out of sleep slowly
Like a flower in slow motion photography;
The petals of your lips
Open to meet mine
And thought is gone,
Erased by this pure
Deep need
That is in our blood and bones.
Your eyes close again.
We will be here longer
Tasting the sweetness
Of this time, even though
I know
That time is not our friend.

DAWN DREAMING

Just before the first
Pale blue light of dawn
When I am me and not me,
Awake and not awake
The gate is open—
My garden is my garden,
The cactus is blooming
For an instant—
And it's not my garden—
There's too much luminous light
In that single drop of water
On the yucca leaf
Where I see my own face reflected
For an instant
And I want to go through the gate.

There are worlds in
That drop of water
Beyond my eyes
Beyond this traveling pain

Worlds of light and music—
Did it rain in the night?
Or am I crying?
I see and I am all this
Before the crushing
Weight of consciousness
Returns and it is time to rise.

MOON AND SEA YOU AND ME

The waters of the sea
Are moved by the moon
Yet the moon does nothing
But be the moon.
I am not the moon
And you are not the sea
I feel and I need and I love
While, moonlike, you are
Only you.

SPACE

This space you left in me
When you left me
Like the northern plains
After a heavy snowstorm,
Is silent and still
Virgin and vast.
The space in me
Your leaving left
Is rough at the edges
And wide and deep
As the way we loved;
It reaches to the edges
Of my soul and beyond.
There is no need for forgiveness,
There is nothing to forgive—
You are free and the love is
Still there, but there is
That empty
You shaped space in me
That nothing else can fill.

LOVE

Love can bend the laws of physics
Love can touch and cleanse your soul
Love is often just an actor
Playing a demanding role.
Love can be a magician
In Vegas creating an illusion
That we love
Even though we know
It's nothing but sweet delusion.
Love can overrule an ego
Love can lead you in the dark
Love can batter, beat and bleed you
Always leaving you it's mark.
Love is like a quick-change artist
Hard to follow, fast to change
Love gives no regrets and no apologies
Love makes no plans that need to change.
Love is yours for the taking
Take the risk, go for a spin
For with love, even when
You lose, you win.

OUR FIRE

All those goodbyes
Have taken their toll,
Yet here you still are,
Camped out in my soul,
Warming yourself
By the fire we ignited
That first time our lips met.
No, do not go,
I'm glad that you came
And please don't forget
To keep feeding that flame.

MAGNETS

You gave your body free rein
And every time it came to me
With no hesitation, no
Misgivings, no second thoughts.
Our bodies always
Chose for us
What we would do, how they
Would spend that love
They generated
We trusted our bodies
And they were always right.

THE WINNER

Go to sleep, my darling
Here next to me—
Our bodies agree
This is where
We should be
No matter what others
Think or say,
Love will win
And when the others
Have all gone away
Leaving nothing behind
With no more words
Left to say,
Love will stay.

THERE WILL BE NO SEQUEL

Go ahead and ride off
Like one of those dubious heroes
In a spaghetti western—
One of those heroes
Who goes unnamed
One of those bad boys
Who just can't be tamed,
Leaving behind a trail
Of tears, blood and corpses
Left to rot in the sun,
Taking with you only your horse
(unnamed too) and your gun.
As the credits roll
Across the screen,
A lonely wind blows
While I watch you go
As tumbleweeds blow
In the wind.

LIFE CAN BE BRUTAL

Though I once valued and loved you
Beyond all the others
Beyond all reason and sense,
I don't think I like
The old man you're become,
That self-proclaimed, unkind
Sad old curmudgeon
Displeased and disgruntled,
Who lives in your mind
In a state of perpetual high dudgeon,
Surrounded by things that you
Valued beyond all other things—
Even me—
Paper things, titles and deeds
To houses and land,
Dollars and cents
In banks and on hand.
Tell me—
Now that you're old
And you say,
Lonely without me—
What do you value now?

DIVORCE LOGIC

You say I deserve
All the misery
You so lavishly
Bestowed on me—
Then I also deserve
This serendipity
That I so happily gained
Upon losing you.

THE NARCISSIST

You betrayed me
Just by living how you live,
Thinking only of yourself,
Taking, taking, taking,
Never anything to give.
Angry, always angry
Never knowing why,
Loving nothing,
Loving no one
No one loving you.
Do you understand
Why you do what you do?
Narcissus sitting
By his pool
Is an amateur
Compared to you.
I wonder if you fell in love
With the splendor
That you think is you,
Would you stare at yourself
Day after day
Until you died too?
No, I wouldn't care.

MY DECLARATION OF INDEPENDENCE

No, I will not wake you—
You come out of sleep
Wearing your anger
 Like a shield,
Your snake eyes
Letting me know
You are ready to strike.
I am unarmed, and alone
 Hiding in plain sight,
 Like a small animal
Trembling in a field
Hoping you will find
A different prey
To feed to your greedy ego,
While I know
I will find a way
A way to get away
Perhaps on a starless
Cloud covered night
When the moon is
Beyond the horizon
Out of our view,
And you will be alone
With no one to care or hurt
And no one to blame but you.

MY PRAYER

Rid me of the pain,
The blame
And this smoldering anger,
And those ideas of love and gain.
Let me live in this lovely now
That won't ever come again.
Make me whole
And holy again.

TO A DOMESTIC TERRORIST

You have been silenced—
Not by the need to be kind
Or the wish to end hate,
But by the sands of time
And the hand of fate.
Still, it's way too late;
I no longer care.

FOR EUGENE

The snows were heavy that winter;
I ran out of wood for my fire
We went to the high south forest
To gather fallen cedar and pine.
I could not help but admire
Your expertise with that axe.

In the spring
 When the winds came,
We drank from the spring
And climbed halfway
Up the mountain
To a cave that gave
Shelter from the wind
And a place for us to rest.
We could see the whole valley below
With the silver ribbon of river
Running through to the west.
Will I ever know
Such peace again?

In September
After the rains

Had replenished the land
You took me to see
Your field of sunflowers
Under the sun and the
Red rock mesas above.
Sunflowers have always been
Something I love-
How could you tell?
When did you learn
To know me so well?

I will remember your beautiful face,
Your light hearted kindness
And your generous soul.
Am I to grow old
Without you?
Will I ever see you again
Or are these memories
All I have left?

A DUET

HIS PART:
Girl, you are surely aware
That it's very rare
For someone to care
About your welfare
Like I do.
So let me advise you-
And this may surprise you
I can no longer disguise
And I won't apologize
I love you
I care
I won't go anywhere
I'll always be there.
I love you.

HER PART;
Boy, yes I could see
You are sweet on me
But don't you see?
It can never be
The only thing
On which we agree

Is, I'm just like you
I love women too
So I will never
Ever be with you.

AT THE SEASHORE

Sleek brown seal
On silver waves
His bright eyes
Search the shore—
And find me.
If I could swim
Through waves so strong
I would meet you
In the sea.

ANOTHER RACE THEORY

The whole concept of race within the human spectrum is not correct. There is only one race, the human race and we all belong to that one race. The differences between us are wonderful and fun and full of surprise and joy, but of little consequence otherwise due to the fact that our similarities are far more important.

We must become like little children who don't give one damn what color anyone is or where they're from or what's in their bank account; the children care only for how someone treats them. Nothing else matters, not language or size or sex or color or history or ANY OTHER THING.

SECTION TWO
STATE OF THE UNION STUFF

GUILT

You can falsify an alibi,
When accused, just deny,
When questioned, don't reply,
Demand your attorney, lie,
But, in the end,
Even if you're president,
You will comply.

ADIOS 2021

That gas-passing fat man
Who sat in the White House,
His mouth spouting foulness
Has finally gone,
And I do not care.
Has anyone counted
The silverware?

YET ANOTHER TRANSLATION

Billions of words
Have been written and spoken
About what Jesus taught.
Kings and philosophers
Madmen and fools
Have written and spoken
About what they think
That he thought.
And yet that message
Could be given
With one four-letter word—
Noun, adjective, adverb and verb.
It all boils down to that one word.
Love. Use it how you choose.

THE STARS

The stars of our galaxy
Speak of ancient spiritual matters
To mankind
In times of darkness.
They speak of
Sacred dimensions:
Grace, guidance,
Inexhaustible knowledge,
Inexpressible joy.

TRY SOMETHING ELSE

The Revolutionary War
Was to rid ourselves
Of the tyranny
Of the monarchy.
The Civil War
Was to rid ourselves
Of the misery
Of slavery.
World War Two
Was to rid ourselves
Of the atrocity
Of Nazi insanity.
The War On Drugs
Was to rid ourselves
Of the toxicity
Of drug dependency.

And yet—

The monarchy,
Although declawed,
Is still here

And the slavery,
Although renamed,
Is still here,
And the Nazis,
Although Neo now
Are still here.
And all the drugs,
Even more than before,
Are still here.
All of which
Should tell us this:
WAR DOES NOT WORK.

BE PATIENT

The 45th administration
With its incompetence and cruelty,
It's corruption and tomfoolery
Its racism and misogyny,
Its bald-faced mendacity
(20,000 lies in four years)
It's total lack of empathy,
(Their motto, "I really don't care, do you?")
Selfishness and white supremacy,
A failed attempt at a coup,
Foolishness and stupidity,
(Let's build a wall,)
Arrogance and mob mentality,
Its out-of-date idiocy,
Its entitled facist hypocrisy,
The list goes on and on,
Tweet after tweet,
But, be patient, all of it
Will one day be reduced
To an asterisk
By history.

WINNERS AND LOSERS

Another billionaire died
After a long battle with greed.
(Greed won.)
He couldn't take those billions with him
Although he really tried.
It seems his widow and his children
Had a great abiding need
So all their many lawyers
Went before the judge to plead.
The judge, in his great wisdom agreed,
 That, yes, indeed,
The old guy in the coffin,
Would not really need
Those piles of dirty money
Where he was headed,
So they pried
Them from his stiffened fingers
And those lawyers won each case
And took that money with them
Leaving just a trace
For the widow and the children
And almost no one cried,
Although some did cry for the billions
And the winner still was greed.

A 21ST CENTURY CAUTIONARY TALE

A horny young college kid,
Gangly and raw
Started a web site
Designed only to draw
Women, lots of women, to him.
Why not give biology
A bit of help from technology?
But it got out of hand
When half of the world
Jumped on his band wagon and
Internet social media,
That haven for crazies, was born.
And the startled young geek
Soon understood clearly
That he had a tiger by its balls
And that tiger was dragging him
Up that proverbial creek.
Like a deer in the headlights,
He appeared before Congress
To try to explain
What the hell had gone wrong.
But nobody knew,
Not even our hero,
And Congress, that haven
For old white men
Past their prime
Still living on the
Taxpayer's dime

Didn't even have the questions to ask,
About how to control
That tiger like beast
Our hapless young genius
Had accidentally unleashed
On the Highway of Misinformation.

SOME QUESTIONS

Have you ever been in love?
Do the stars belong to you?
Can you pole vault over rainbows
Or count the many shades of blue?

Do you long to be forgiven?
Do you wish to learn to fly?
Leave your body on the seashore
And soar into the sky?

Have you ever kept a secret
Or drank from the Milky Way?
Do you ever think of childhood
When you still knew how to play?

Can you calm the raging storms?
Dance naked in the rain?
Can you hear the angels sing?
Can you tell insane from sane?

Do you pray that all religion
Will implode and die away
 And from those ashes will arise
A new and better way?

If you had seen Baby Hitler
In his cradle
And you knew
What he would do,
Do you think that killing him
Would have been
The proper thing to do?

MORE QUESTIONS

Our love was forbidden
As love often is—
Why is hate not forbidden?
Although we tried
There was no way to hide
The love we felt and shared—
Why does no one hide hate?
We censor love scenes
And watch a thousand
Brutal murders on our screens.
Is humanity perverted?
Why is so much time spent
Justifying hate
While love is always justified?
No questions needed.

GRAVITY

Gravity
Is a mystery
To me.
Is it just scotch tape
Holding things in place
Or does it have another face?

Some people say
That this world
And all that
It can reveal
Is nothing but illusion
Held together in God's mind,
So gravity
Is no mystery
Because nothing
Here is real.

And some people say
God's a giant Being
In whom we move and live,
So all we are
And all we have
Is that Being's
Gift to give,
And the mystery
Is that gravity
Is the blood pressure
Of our Host.

You can choose
And believe
Whatever theory
You like the most
Or make one of your own.

REQUIEM FOR A THIEF
(MAYBE OUR THIEF IN CHIEF)

Fantasy is all that's left for your soul
After a lifetime of counting coup on
Those from whom you stole
All your dubious golden treasure.
Do you really think you've won
When there's so little left to measure
Now that the ending bell has rung
And there's no one left to care
And no one cries or says a prayer?
Did you finally learn
You can't keep what you steal?
Did you really think
Your fantasy was real?

ANOTHER QUESTION I DON'T HAVE THE ANSWER TO

Because life is eternal
And we all live our lives
On a Mobius Strip
Déjà vu is always true.
We have done it all before
Somewhere
Sometime.
The question then is this:
How do we get off the Strip?

21ST CENTURY AMERICAN LAMENT

We walk through
Fields of poppies
Our only aim
Is to ease the pain
Of not achieving
Our only goal—
To be a billionaire
On the dole
Courtesy of the working masses
Who barely have enough to eat.
We've learned their lesson
Of how to cheat,
But it isn't working—
What is wrong?
No help for us
But the poppies
Now that all the
Dreams are gone.
We see all our idols falling
One by lonely one,
Indictments handed down
Like popcorn

Lost at sea
In a storm
Of greed and meanness—
This has now become the norm.
So lie down in
Your field of poppies
Dream your dreams
Of escape.
Those billionaires
That you envy
Can't take it with them
Even on their trips to space.

MIDNIGHT RAMBLING

Am I who I think I am?
Or someone or something else?
Is there more to this life
Than I see on the edge
Where I live?
Am I missing the point?
Is there a point to miss?
The answers must be yes;
There is too much unknown
For the answers to be no.

DO NOT TURN AWAY

I saw a hungry child today
Do not turn away-
I thought of my own chubby
Little children at play-
Do not turn away.

I saw photos of a hurricane today-
Do not turn away-
Tearing up someone's life
Blowing it away-
Do not turn away.

I saw hopeful people walk
Two thousand miles today-
Do not turn away-
Looking for a better life-
Do not turn away.

I saw a homeless man today-
Do not turn away-
I thought of my home
With windows and walls,
And doors that lock
And a yard where
My chubby children play.
Do not turn away.

AURORA BOREALIS

Just below the pine covered hills
On the Montana line
On a fearsome cold winter night,
Grandpa said, "Come look,"
And there in the sky
Were ribbons of light
That moved and danced
In a deep blue sky.
There was no wind
And no snow;
It was twenty below.
Nothing moved but those lights—
We could see all the way
To our own Milky Way
Beyond those northern lights.
Science says:
Storms that rage
Across the face of the sun
Throw showers of bright
Living particles
Onto the earth
At two million
 Miles per hour.
They crash into our
Magnetic field
And give birth
To the northern lights.
That's probably true,
As far as it goes.

If I got it right.
The North people say:
It's their ancestors
Who have become pure light.
They come back in the night
And I think that's right,
We're all made of light,
But there could be
Something more.
Those curtains of light
Could be a door
To the other side.
Pull those curtains aside
And then tell me
What you see.

TALKING HEADS 2021

Misinformed miscreants
Want to take over,
Spouting their lies
On Washington's Pravda,
Their mouths always open
Like assholes abloom,
All of them packing
And all of them lacking
A soul.

NOTES FROM THE PSYCH WARD

The vultures are circling
Out there in the desert;
I know they're coming,
They're coming for me.
My brother called them.
My brother's my keeper
He's a light sleeper
But not a deep thinker,
His best friend's the Grim Reaper
And he's also a sweeper
Of many things under the rug.
I know if I had one,
He'd pull the plug.
I know I'm quite unusual,
He says paranoid delusional
And that I have chosen to
Live in my own La La Land,
Peopled by spirits
Both evil and tame.
Well, so be it then.
I won't live in his macho world
Where his male dominant flags

Are always unfurled;
Where he sleeps all curled
Up in the fetal position,
Still living off blood of women
Like the vampire he is.
So it's back to the psych ward
For more observation
And some consternation.
I think I'll hit on my shrink.
What do you think?
Anyway, that's my plan.
You have to get your love
Wherever you can.
The vultures have landed
They're tearing my flesh—
There, in that mirror,
Is that my face?
Or has someone else
Taken my place?

GENERATION GAP

Mama didn't twerk
Daddy didn't do cocaine
Mama went to church
Daddy used the booze
To fry his brain.

MORE QUESTIONS

How do you choose a one-night stand
Or does a one-night stand choose you?
How do you choose a lifetime mate
Or someone with whom to procreate?
How do you know falling in love
Won't become falling in hate?
Is it just biology?
Or random chaos driven by need?
Is it runaway chemistry
Or programmed reproduction?
Maybe even love?
All of the above?
And will I ever know?
Even the Bible admits
Some things remain a mystery
That are never to be
Understood.
The way of a man with a maid
Is one of these mysteries.
So does anybody know?
Those eight billion people out there
Tell me we're doing it all the time-
So why doesn't someone know?

TO THE BILLIONAIRES

You've been sucking so long
At Mother Earth's breast
Taking way more
So all of the rest
Of us are now
The runts of the litter
Feeling quite bitter
Toward all of you.
How can you be so rude
So lacking in gratitude
Don't you know
There are children out there
Without any food?
You're riding rockets to space
But not to better
The human race,
Most likely to get your face
On everyone's TV.
What do you want
For your legacy?
Something good
Or these ridiculous tales
Of idiocy?

You're on public welfare
And you don't seem to care
About where
Those funds are coming from.
You pay little tax
And that is a fact
While the rest of us toil
To support you.
So, go ahead, buy the world,
Leave your self-flag unfurled
On every square inch of earth
Charge us all rent
Pat yourself on the back
Keep bragging about
What you're worth.
The next time you spend
Those millions to send
A rocket to circle the sun
For ten thousand years or more,
Don't send it unmanned
You go along too
We'll all applaud you,
But there will be no tears.
You've chosen your path
Now deal with the wrath
Of all of us here below you

While your ship
Turns to rust
And you turn to dust,
Everyone else will finally
Get something from you,
A great belly laugh.

WINTER BLIZZARD

There are lights
Along the highway
Here and there
Haloed by the
Swirling snow.
Windshield wipers drag
Heavy with the
Wet snowflakes.
Do you think we'll
Make it home?

REFLECTIONS

Where the river idles peaceful
It mirrors shore and sky,
Then dainty ripples break the scene
In a lovely Seurat summer scene;
And then, downstream,
The swirling water rapids
Erase reflected shore and sky
Until all you see
Is the troubled water.
In the same way, you and I
Have troubles that obscure the reality
Of the reflection
Of our own Divine Perfection.

LESSONS WE CAN LEARN FROM THE FALL OF EMPIRES

I was thinking about the America of the 21st century, so I googled the end of empires and I learned this:

1. The Viking Empire ended due to social change; looting wasn't profitable anymore.
   LESSON: the economy IS important.

2. The fall of the Mongol Empire was due to sibling rivalry among Genghis Khan's unruly grandkids.
   LESSON: You can't rule if you're unruly.

3. The Roman Empire fell due to internal corruption and military losses to barbarians.
   LESSON: You can't sit around getting drunk and eating tongues of nightingales at orgies while surrounded by barbarians without losing your empire.

4. The Russian Empire fell due to war and corruption like Rome and all those others.
   LESSON: Control yourself.

5. The Empire of Cyrus the Great was taken down by a lady warrior of the Steppes.
   LESSON: Never underestimate a woman warrior.

6. The fall of the Empire of Alexander the Great was due to the untimely death of Alex himself and the Black Plague that killed almost everyone else.

LESSON: You can't keep an empire going if you're all dead.

7. The Greek Empire ended due to civil wars between city states.
LESSON: In house fighting can take you down. Ask any divorce attorney.

8. The Egyptian Empire ended due to climate change and volcanic activity.
LESSON: You can't keep an empire going with lava and ash raining down during floods and hurricanes, tsunamis and typhoons.

9. The Assyrian Empire ended because it got too big and impossible to control.
LESSON: you must control yourself and your empire.

10. The Qing Dynasty ended due to new technology and rebellion.
LESSON: Maybe we should heed Stephen Hawking's warning about AI.

11. The Abased Caliphate and the Achaemenid of the First Persian Empire (who?) ended due to Genghis Khan.
LESSON: See item 2. Patience is necessary.

12. The Ottoman Empire ended due to economic problems. The deficit got too big.
LESSON: You can't run an empire if you're broke.

13. The Maurya Empire ended due to weak leadership.
LESSON: Think 45th president of the US.

14. The Yuan Dynasty and Umayyad Caliphate ended due to peasant revolution.
LESSON: Hungry, homeless people just might get

pissed. Think French Revolution and those baskets full of heads.

15. The British Empire was taken down by a little guy in a diaper who practiced passive resistance.
LESSON: Beware of peace? And Love? Yes, do.

How odd than in all that googling, there was no mention of stupidity as a cause of the downfall of empires, which is strange considering that it is becoming more and more apparent that the American Experiment/Empire could likely go down due to widespread, unbridled, underestimated Stupidity.
LESSON: Beware of stupidity. It can be deadly.

SECTION THREE
WORLD OF WOMEN

I RODE SHOTGUN

I rode shotgun,
Never got to drive,
Took a back seat,
Played second fiddle;
I was second class,
Second best, second choice.
I was Eve, bringer of evil,
I was the Whore of Babylon,
Destroyer of man.
And I was used to it;
This was my birthright—
I didn't even have my own name,
I was called woMAN, feMALE,
And I had to take his name.
NOW...
I make my own choices,
Choose my own place
Find my own home.
I am no longer second in my mind.
If I am still second in your mind,
Change it.

MARRIAGE

I'm tired of reaping
What you sow
Because I'm chained to you
Like that movie in which
The two guys are chained
To each other running for
Their lives as bullets
Zing by their heads.
Yes, it has become that
Dramatic and one of us
Is that stupid.
I'm at the point
Where I would choose that bullet
If it removed those chains and you.

JUST ANOTHER KAREN

She likes her grapes peeled
And her court records sealed;
She's entitled and don't you forget it.
Her daddy's well heeled
(Grandpa knew how to steal)
So don't you dare cross her
Or you will regret it.

She wears lots of Dior
And has boyfriends galore
All of whom claim to adore
Her, until they just can't ignore
How she only adores
Herself and they finally get it.

She will wind up alone,
She will wail and bemoan,
Blame everyone else
And never quite get it.
She's just another Karen.

ON LOWERING THE DIVORCE RATE

Since marriage is the
Main cause of divorce
And, Like the chastity belt,
Is now obsolete,
Marriage, like the eight-track tape,
Needs to go away.
Please don't panic, all of you
Out there in the Bible Belt.
God did not invent marriage—
Men did, to keep track
Of their stuff and their sperm;
The pharaohs married their sisters,
Royalty married its cousins
While eunuchs guarded harems
To keep the women pure.
Not a good thing for the eunuchs either.
But now we have a better way
That God did invent,
Who's your daddy now
Is solved by DNA.

IT'S ALL RELATIVE

Piss is onomatopoeia at its best
Say all the little boys.
Hush say all the grandmas.

EARTH IS FEMALE TOO

Aristotle said this:
Woman is the supreme example
Of the failure of form to
Dominate matter.
Really, Dude? I am appalled
At the gall of such idle chatter
When I consider the mess
Men have made while they reigned
As Lord and Master
Of our lovely blue world.
You have laid waste to the land.
What will it take
To make you understand
That balance needs to be restored?
You need women.
Will you learn this before
The last war begins?
I fear this:
It won't be long
Before the Earth burns
And your need for destruction
Takes over and
The last shred of love is gone.

YOU ARE KNOWN BY THE COMPANY YOU KEEP

Two old women
Wandered by us,
Their faces altered
And frozen
By the knife,
Botoxed within an
Inch of their life.
If you really wanted
To make us think
You were still young,
You should have come alone.
Those two old men
With wrinkled cheeks
And drooping eyes
Following behind you
Should have been left at home.

LIFE ON EARTH

Life on earth is precarious. We live on a great ball of fire (sorry, Jerry Lee, I had to steal that from you) covered with dirt and rocks and water in a ratio of three parts water to one part dirt. Curiously, it is said that our bodies conform to that same ratio.

And all of that water and dirt over that ball of fire, which is heated by an even bigger ball of fire, is held together by a force someone called gravity, even though no one seems to know what gravity is while the whole thing turns around on its axis like a whirling dervish making one turn every 24 hours.

Our world, this wonderful ball, makes a trip around the sun once a year at about 6000 miles per hour.

Our fiery world is a dangerous place. And now there are about 8 billion of us humans living on this speeding ball of fire and a whole lot of them are angry and fighting, desperate and crazy, so:

TO WHOEVER OR WHATEVER IS OUT THERE: HELP! WE NEED HELP!!

SECTION FOUR
21ST CENTURY SONNETS

SONNET # ONE

My hands remember the shape of your face
My fingers know the texture of your hair
My fear was that you'd leave without a trace.
My words of love to you were like a prayer,
A prayer to keep you safe right here with me.
My arms still feel how they felt around you
I hear the words of love you gave to me.
I wonder, can you hear those love words too?
I hear your voice in sweet dreams as I sleep
My lips still taste the sweetness of your kiss
I see your face through my tears as I weep;
I still smell that after shave that I miss
My body's cells were rearranged by you,
Now that you are gone, what am I to do?

SONNET # TWO

All those untapped powers within us all
Come to the fore whenever you are near
It does not matter if you hear or call
That bond is stronger than the hate or fear.
Yes, my beloved, I will always hear
I sense your voice no matter where I go
In noise or silence, whether far or near;
I would not say this if it weren't so.
Though life circumstances tore you away,
You did not leave my heart, my mind and soul.
Although I could not ask for you to stay,
Yet, here you are, still keeping my heart whole.
I saw the sun rise in its majesty
And I called your name so that you could see.

SONNET # THREE

Almost every day I'm thinking of you
When summer's on the desert and it's hot
My thought still remains the same—I love you.
Spring and fall, it's all the same—all I've got.
Though the wild passion we shared is now gone
What remains is now deeper, soft and warm,
Faded like the last notes of a love song.
I love the peace after that raging storm.
In the winter, when I sit by the fire
Dreaming of your touch, lost in memory,
Wondering how you are, who sits by your fire,
My thoughts are, for me, enough company.
If I could, I wonder if I would trade
Those thoughts for just one day of love we made.

SONNET # FOUR

Our love was almost like insanity;
We were afraid we might kill each other,
The passion was so strong, so heavenly,
I knew I could never love another
With the same kind of pure, intense longing
That would only abate when you touched me
Which made all of my cells begin singing.
Yet I feared you would be taken from me.
In all those years, we never disagreed;
The love we shared gave us comfort and peace.
What more could any human ever need?
And yet, I knew in time, that it would end
And I was right. You had to go away.
But that passionate love was here to stay.

SONNET # FIVE

Our bodies fit together perfectly,
Every inch, every surface, every line
As though they were made by some Diety
Who knew that love was there in that design.
Like heroin you said, can't get enough
We're lost in clouds with mirrors and some smoke.
With love like this, we knew we must be tough,
For love like this can kill you with one stroke.
That fierce passion nearly tore us in two,
But it was followed by comfort and peace,
And knowing it was the right thing to do,
We cherished our short time of sweet release.
That dark wild passion might someday be gone,
But that deep love and comfort will live on.

SONNET # SIX

My love for you is not negotiable
You do not have to say any I dos
I won't put you on any pedestal
You will always have the right to refuse.
My love accepts, you do not have to change
You are as you are and that is just right,
There is nothing I want to rearrange;
There will not be any reason to fight.
My love is free, there is no quid pro quo.
No rules, no lawyers, no extraction plan;
If you choose to leave, I will watch you go.
I will hide my tears from you if I can.
Love is not love if it seeks to hold on,
This love will stay even when you have gone.

SONNET # SEVEN

The monumental task of living right
Was given us before our day of birth.
Like the plants, we must turn toward the light;
Be like the trees who practice peace on earth
And give their fruits to anyone who's there,
While asking only for earth, sun and rain,
Their every breath a lovely form of prayer,
Needing nothing so there's no need for gain.
Plants are far more diverse than humans are,
Yet they see no race, class, no religion.
They're more content than humans are, by far,
And when they worship, they worship the sun.
If I could choose what plant I want to be,
I'd be a tough desert dweller like me.

SONNET # EIGHT
MIDNIGHT HOPELESSNESS

Those ranting, raving, screaming maniacs
Who live in my head need to be quiet,
They are wild and feral, running in packs,
Waiting, hoping to start a great riot.
Did I let them move in and take over?
Do I need the sheriff to evict them?
Does my whole psyche need a makeover?
Can I get a jury to convict them?
I could get a priest for an exorcism
Or ask Jesus to cast them into swine.
Living like this is being imprisoned;
My mind is theirs, it is no longer mine.
My psychiatrist quit, and then he cried,
"There's no help for you, commit suicide!"

SONNET # NINE
CHANGES

Mama Earth has gone through many changes
From one celled creatures to self-aware man.
Earthquakes have pushed up our mountain ranges;
Did this just happen or is there a plan?
Dentalium shells we found on the plain
Tell us an ocean once covered the land;
Was this an accident or was it planned?
Rivers carved canyons through hard solid rock;
It took centuries to create all this,
Whatever did it is not on the clock,
We think we see it, but what did we miss?
Life is eternal, so change is required,
So that we and God don't get bored and tired.

SONNET # TEN
LOSS

You should not have abandoned me, my love,
Leaving me lonely with no more to lose.
I forgave you, but when push comes to shove,
Remember that I, too, can always choose
To wait or move on, to live or to die.
You ran away, but I still had to stay
To clean up that mess, at least give a try,
To reap what we sowed, it won't go away.
I never blamed you, the love didn't go,
But how could I ever trust you again?
The years went by and I went with the flow
Wondering and waiting, hoping and then—
You called and wanted me to come to you,
But it was something I just could not do.

SONNET # ELEVEN
LIVING ON THE LINE

Once again, I'm on the line of scrimmage
Waiting impatiently for the next play.
In this bloody war that some call marriage,
Call a time out so we live one more day.
You've taken my time, my physical self;
Now you tell me you're after my soul—
Please, be quiet, put me back on the shelf.
I can't last much longer, it's fourth and goal.
You appointed the kids as referee
So you're quarterback, coach and owner too,
It's your field, your ball, nothing left for me.
What is it that you expect me to do?
My contract is void, I want to retire,
Before I set this stadium on fire.

SONNET # TWELVE
OMENS AND DREAMS

A murder of crows sat in the dead tree
That stood by the road that led to my gate.
The people said that omen was for me
That I should run before it was too late.
I had a dream that my love had returned
And the crows came there just to celebrate.
My love wants to tell me what he has learned;
He is so afraid it might be too late.
"No, you must run," all the old women cried,
"that murder of crows is a bad, dark sign.
You know that your lover always has lied."
I know that is true. He was never mine,
So that murder of crows got their own way.
I cried as I packed, but I went away.

ATTENTION SPANS

I heard someone say that our average attention span is now three minutes. We can't focus on anything more than three minutes at a time?

I heard it on TV, which has programmed me to focus for three minutes or less, on commercials for stuff I don't need, so maybe I didn't hear all of it.

Three minutes? You can't even make an omelet in three minutes. I've had longer fights than that with a family member over whether I cooked that omelet right.

This can't be right. If it is, we'll never have another Romeo and Juliet, not even a remake. We'll never have another Taj Mahal or Golden Gate Bridge or Mona Lisa if it's true.

No, it can't be true. We may be slow learners or even in the dumb group, and we are obviously on the edge of a massive change in society, from the industrial age to the age of information, but we are resilient and the young ones are smart. It can't be true. It takes more than three minutes to smoke a joint, sex should take more than three minutes. It even takes more than three minutes to take a pee and wash your hands, so I won't worry too much; no more than three minutes at least.

SECTION FIVE
HAIKU AND SENRYU

TIME

You brought me flowers
But it was half past too late
Flowers won't fix this.

DIVINE RIGHT?

The royal family
Seems quite unremarkable
Is royalty a scam?

HOMO SAPIENS

With savage vengeance
We kill the best among us
Then pretend we're right.

LEMONS, LEMONS, LEMONS

It occurs to me
That I've had to make too much
Goddamn lemonade.

CLUES

I've got a feeling
You don't love me anymore
Since you fired that shot.

JANUARY 2021

May the madness end
And the would-be dictator
Go. Live, die, but go.

LOVE

I long to see you
And touch you and hold you now—
Just for a moment

LOVE

You left me when I
Most needed you. I survived.
Now I don't need you.

CLICHES

"I'm just killing time,"
Said the people. Then time said,
"It's reciprocal."

THE LINE'S NOT BUSY

Why is it that calls
To the Lurdanite hotline
Are never answered?

THEY'RE ALL MADE UP

We need a new word
For chili cooking contests
It's groupenfarten.

LOVE

Love is a mirage
Shimmering and fiery
Full of fire and hope.

ADVICE

They said forget him
But I cannot forget you
Even though I die.

THE SYCOPHANT

Stripped of your power
You are just another fool
Licking the wrong boots.

NARCISSITIC PERSONALITY DISORDER

It's all about you
No one else even matters
You will be alone.

MORE NPD

If reality
Does not meet your ego need,
Of course, you must lie.

LOVE

I do love haiku
It is minimalism
In poetic form.

LOVE

Take your mask off, Boy
Show me who you really are,
Will I still love you?

REINCARNATION

Reincarnation
Answers so many questions
That one life does not.

MARRIAGE

She died in harness
Yoked to a fool who seldom
Noticed she was there.

21ST CENTURY AFFLUENZA

In America
Even the dogs and cats are
Lazy, soft and fat.

LOVE

Meeting my lover
My heart beats so very wild
I think I might die.

DO THE MATH

It's better to give
Than to receive, but I say
They are both equal.

DO THE MATH (TWO)

Without receivers
There can be no givers, so
They are both equal.

LOVE

You have within you
The most precious gifts of all:
Peace, love happiness.
 --Jesus-

SOAPS TOO

Telenovelas
Are extreme, wild, unlikely,
But so is real life.

LOVE

Savage tenderness
Between us nearly kills me.
I'm okay with that.

LOVE

Go to sleep, darling
Don't fret about the ending
Of love that went wrong.

ILLUSION

There are strings of light
Hanging from a hot night sky.
Have I lost my mind?

CONFUSION

I saw you last night
In a dream within a dream
Is anything real?

2020- ME TOO

In the pandemic
Most everyone wrote a book
I don't want to read.

HEALTH CARE PLAN

The lame, halt and blind
All at my doctor's office
Jesus, we need you.

ELECTION 2020

We are overjoyed
The president is gone now
Long live our country.

WHITE SUPREMACY?

If you believe that
White skin is superior
Why use bottled tan?

OR MONEY

That elephant in
Your room is so often sex
In one of its forms.

POLITICS

A dynasty of
Fools, liars, thieves and con men
Will destroy us all.

MORE POLITICS

Gerrymandering,
Voter suppression and hate
Brought us a monster.

LOVE

I want to lie down
In your arms in a field of
Marijuana buds.

URINOLOGY 101

You're always pissed off
You say you're always pissed on
That's way too much piss.

NO TWO ALIKE

We are like snowflakes
None are exactly alike
That is wonderful.

RELIGION

If Jesus came back
He would still not be Christian
They became too mean.

RELIGION 101

The really righteous
Don't speak of it; the self
Righteous always do.

ANOTHER 110 DEGREE DAY

Leaves droop in the sun
A hot breeze blows from the south
August in Phoenix.

SOS

Unspeakable things
Gnaw at my bones. In silence,
In loss and in pain.

PHILOSOPHY 101

Innocence and guilt
Diametrically opposed?
Maybe, maybe not.

MORE SOS

It's four A. M. and
I'm awake, angry and sad.
I really need help.

OBVIOUSLY

I don't want to be
A liar. I will not lie.
I can't be a spy.

LOVE ETC.

I carried that torch
Until it burned my body
Back to sanity.

MARRIAGE

He attached himself
Like a barnacle to me
Consuming my soul.

POLITICS

The King is insane
Sending troops to our cities
We have to kill him.

MORE LOVE

Violence and love
Do not belong together.
They are not the same.

RAIN

It rained this morning,
A short, soft, sweet winter rain—
The plants are grateful.

MAYBE

Dire straits is my street
And I chose it for myself.
I may be insane.

CITY SOUNDS

Tires on the pavement
Heartbeat of the symphony-
The city's motor.

A QUESTION

Hazy memories
That don't quite fit together-
Can this life be real?

MAYBE OVERTIME

It's time to admit
I know next to nothing of
Damn near everything.

SOME OF IT MINE

Thanks to God for clothes-
There's a lot of naked skin
I don't want to see.

THEOLOGY 101

"You only live once,"
The wise woman said to me,
"But it's forever."

DIVORCE

You ransacked my soul
And took all that you wanted
Leaving a wasteland.

THEOLOGY 101

Heaven's not a place
Heaven is a state of mind
You can go there now.

MORE THEOLOGY

The eternal flame
Of love within all of us
Is fragile. Don't blow.

I'M WITH STUPID

You believed the lies,
You did what the tyrant asked;
You're in jail, he's free.

PHILOSOPHY 101

If you are confused
About the meaning of life,
Then you are human.

POLITICS

The ex-president
Is feeding off the rotting
Corpse of his dead dreams.

OR A LION

If I was a snake
I would surely have bit you
A long time ago.

SOS

I was born too soon
Or maybe it was too late,
I don't belong here.

RELIGION

The terrorist said,
"I did it for the Prophet,"
Or was it profit?

EASILY AND OFTEN

Ignorance is bliss?
Ignorance and misery
Can live together.

PEACE

Peace is possible
It is within all of us,
It belongs to us.

JANUARY 6, 2021

White supremacy?
Yet here you are, armed, acting
Like an animal.

SHOPPING

I love thrift stores where
Those with cash, but no taste
Throw away treasures.

TURN OVER THOSE MONEY TABLES

Those nutcase Christians
Are still worshipping idols:
Televangelists.

DUST BUNNIES?

We are made of dust,
The dust of our Mother Earth
We are holy dust.

DARWIN WAS RIGHT

Stuff comes and stuff goes,
Dodo birds and hula hoops
Evolution stays.

I STOLE THIS FROM CICERO. SORRY

Our biggest mistake:
Taking from others instead
Of making our own.

THE TRUTH WILL SET YOU FREE

You're just a bundle
Of addictions—and sadly
One of them was me.

DAWN

The shadows of birds
Fly across my sunlit wall.
Time for me to rise.

LOVE

I do love drag queens
Because I'm a woman and
They do love women.

EINSTEIN SAID IT (OR SOMETHING LIKE IT)

Imagination
Is the best indication
Of intelligence

LET US SPEAK THIS INTO EXISTENCE

Out of date evils—
Slavery, misogyny
Are now history.

WHITE SUPREMACY, FALLACIES, IDIOCIES AND TRUTH

Kipling was wrong, but
Right. There's a white man's burden.
His stupidity.

LOVE

In San Francisco
You bought me a gardenia.
I can smell it still.

LOVE

Sunshine and shadow-
Our love is tender and fierce,
Delicate and strong.

THE LEADER

How can you guide me
When you are lost in fog dreams
That you think are real?

ILLUSION

Good versus evil
Is part of the dream mirage-
There is only good.

GRATITUDE

How can I thank you
For your help, your care, your love?
Words are not enough.

GO AWAY

You are a heavy,
Wet, stinking blanket that lays
Over all our joy.

THINK FOR YOURSELF

"Question everything,"
My meditation teacher
Said. "Find your own truth."

A QUESTION

How could you leave me?
Was it because my husband
Said he would kill you?

21ST CENTURY POLITICS

The republican
Party is on its deathbed
Hallucinating.

DICTATORS

Hitler and Putin
Mussolini and Stalin
Have now all been Trumped.

POLITICS

Pasty old white men
Sit in the senate living
In Yesterdayland.

VOLTAIRE SAID IT TOO

Slartibartfast said:
Find something you love to do
And then just do it.

ANOTHER QUESTION

If I'm not ruthless
  And I don't think I am,
Does that make me ruth?

MORE PHILOSOPHY

If life isn't full
Of sacrifice and helping,
You're doing it wrong.

TO A CONGRESSMAN

You hide behind words
Yet what you are is screaming
Louder than your words.

LOVE

Ashes of our love
Are stirring like the Phoenix
Ready for rebirth.

RACE THEORY

Ideas of race
Are fallacious, there's only
One, the human race.

E=MC2

Since the universe
Can be explained by numbers,
That gives me comfort

SEX

Other people's sex lives
Are not my jurisdiction
So do who you choose.

GIVE ME A MEMORY I CAN USE
-ADELE-

I want to kiss you-
Those deep swollen love kisses
That left me breathless.

TRANS-PORTATION

Do you remember
Those nights we spent together
When we left the earth?

LOVE

I could not have loved
You more-I was enraptured
By you and your love.

LOVE

Each night before sleep
I surround you with white light
So you will be safe.

LOVE

I picture your face,
Your wonderful face that I
Touched so tenderly.

MY PRAYER

Surround my loved ones
With sacred white light of love
And give us all peace.

FOOD

Those who swim with sharks
And think they can tame the beasts
Are often eaten.

CHANGES

There was a time when
Actors were considered trash;
Now we worship them.

PROTECTION

My bougainvillea
Blooms ferociously just like
Its dangerous thorns.

EQUIVOCATION

"It's complicated."
Everyone always says this
When they want to lie.

MARRIAGE

You tried to choke me
Now you want me to love you?
What is wrong with you?

BORDERS

The world needs fengshuied,
Borders obliterated,
Setting us all free.

THANK YOU, TREES

There's a paper trail
Leading all the way from you
To the nearest jail.

MUSIC

Music is sacred
Not just the hymns and the psalms,
But all the music.

FOURTH OF JULY

I love my freedom
To write, to speak and to be
Whatever I choose.

MORE FOURTH OF JULY

You said you own me—
A marriage license is not
Like a bill of sale.

MORE FOURTH OF JULY

Freedom is fragile
And tyrants are everywhere
So be vigilant.

MORE FOURTH OF JULY

Our ex-president
Our racist, rapist-in-chief
Should be in prison.

MORE FOURTH OF JULY

I'm impervious
To your tantrums, your mean streak,
I am free of you.

MORE FOURTH OF JULY

Nuclear winter
Lurks behind all of our eyes-
Do not allow it.

CITIES

Our great cities are
Tons of concrete, glass and steel,
Fragile as freedom.

OUR BLUE WORLD

Globalization
Became inevitable
When we went to space.

OUR WORLD

The world is perfect
So mathematically perfect-
There must be a God.

THE USA 21ST CENTURY

We are a nation
Of lawyers and victims, all
Suing each other.

THE WORLD 21ST CENTURY

National anthem?
No, we need a world anthem,
We are just one tribe.

OUR CAMPFIRE SUN

We are just one tribe
Huddled around our campfire
We must live this truth.

SUN WORSHIPERS

Our sun is on fire
That's what keeps us all alive
We are the sun clan.

SECURITY

When you feel secure
In your made-up little world,
That's when change will come.

AND B.S. TOO

Male supremacy?
And white supremacy too?
That's all just hogwash.

USA 21ST CENTURY

When all of the news
Sounds like Saturday Night Live
We are in trouble

MORE USA 21ST CENTURY

When reality
Begins to sound like satire,
We are in trouble.

MORE USA 21ST CENTURY

When leaders are fools
And followers follow them-
You figure it out.

THINK FOR YOURSELF

Question everything
Do not blindly believe things
You don't understand.

TEN OF THEM?

Heavy stone tablets?
Not even Moses would lug
Them down a mountain.

REALITY 101

Gather ye rosebuds?
Better get a goddamn job
Rosebuds won't feed you.

MORE REALITY

Sabotage myself?
Do not be ridiculous-
Pass me the oxy.

THE LITTLE ONES

Children draw the sun
Because they know where their next
Meal is coming from.

PROGRESS??

Profiting from war
Is an old occupation.
Now we could all die.

USA 21ST CENTURY

You could be my child
You there, rooting through that trash
Hungry and alone.

USA 21ST CENTURY

That rug that we swept
Everything under is now
A mountain of shit.

CAPITALISM 101

The profit motive
Can be an unholy whore,
Wasteful and evil.

TIME TRAVEL

Hubbell's telescope
Revealed the universe is
Violent and vast.

USA 21ST CENTURY

I'm flabbergasted,
Gobsmacked, appalled, disgusted
By Republicans.

USA 21ST CENTURY

Hitch your wagon to
A Hitler-loving facist
And see what happens.

DESMOND TUTU 2021

What a great loss we
We suffered with your passing,
O, great holy one.

REPLACEMENT THEORY

Do not worry, dudes;
Your brand of stupid hate is
Irreplaceable.

AGAIN?

Every time I trace
The source of all my troubles
It is always me.

FROM THE IDIOT'S HANDBOOK

Personal danger
Is not a stranger to me.
I seem to choose it.

DAYBREAK

Streaks of bright red light
Spill across the eastern sky-
The sun is bleeding.

GAMBLERS ANONYMOUS-HEADS UP

Online sports betting?
You can ruin your life and
Never leave your couch.

LOVE

Sex can be sublime
With angels guarding the night
Love makes it holy.

A QUESTION

You live in cages
My sisters in blue burkas,
Do you want freedom?

TO A COWBOY

She tried to love you
But Man, that boot on her neck
Just would not let her.

GLOBALIZATION

Give us humans time
We just barely figured out
Our Earth is a globe.

THE OLYMPICS

Qualifications
For the luge are: fearlessness
And insanity.

MEMORIES

It's snowing tonight
As I sit here by the fire
Remembering you.

AT FIRST SIGHT

Your favorite book
Is the Dictator's Handbook
I do not like you.

EGO TRIPPING

Get out of your way,
Your self-importance is vast
It's holding you back.

IMPOSTER

He rode a white horse
Like in the fairy tales, but
No hero was he.

FORREST GUMP'S MOM WAS RIGHT

Stupidity is
Another word for evil.
Try to avoid it.

TEQUILA WISDOM

The source of my pain
Turns out to be me. Oh, hell!
What am I to do?

VIEWPOINTS

What you are calling
Serendipity might be
The sweet grace of God.

BUT IT'S YOUR DUST AND YOUR CHICKENS

The dust has settled
The chickens came home to roost
Still, it's not my fault

THE TRUTH

When you tell the truth
Sometimes you sound retarded
But that is okay.

RELIGION

Ancestor worship?
Sounds like a good idea.
We owe them so much.

SECTION SIX
SIX WORD STORIES

21ST CENTURY POLITICS

Trump won. Shit.
Trump lost. Shit.

21ST CENTURY LOVE

Got matching tattoos.
Split up. Ouch.

THE WANT ADS

For sale:
Used gun
Owner dead.

SPORTS

First skydive;
Parachute failed.
Last skydive.

GAMBLING

Won lottery.
Bought fentanyl.
Died rich.

SPORTS

Olympic gold.
Used drugs.
Medal gone.

LOVE

Poisoned him. Jail.
Now I'm free.

THE END

Kurt Vonnegut said back in the 1970's that it looked like all of the people who had ever lived were back on Earth for the grand finale.

And there are also all those evangelical and fundamentalist Christian people who have been predicting the End for centuries. Their version involves them and all those who believe exactly like them being taken up into heaven while all us sinners writhe in agony, burning in hell forever as we watch their ascent.

I prefer Kurt Vonnegut's theory because it's not only kinder, but more fun and it doesn't involve eternal hell and damnation. Does it seem odd to you that the people of the church they claim Jesus started do exactly the opposite of what he told them to do?

Our Earth, solar system and galaxy don't seem to be on their deathbed yet. The end still isn't near, unless we bring it about, so please, let's don't do that.

THE END

www.ingramcontent.com/pod-product-compliance
Ingram Content Group UK Ltd.
Pitfield, Milton Keynes, MK11 3LW, UK
UKHW041953230426
12048UKWH00008B/314